BREEDERS' BEST
A KENNEL CLUB BOOK™

Rottweiler

By Victor Clemente

BREEDERS' BEST

A KENNEL CLUB BOOK™

ROTTWEILER

ISBN: 1-59378-912-9

Copyright © 2004

Kennel Club Books, LLC
308 Main Street, Allenhurst, NJ 07711 USA
Printed in South Korea

PHOTOS BY:
Bernd Brinkmann and
Isabelle Français.

DRAWINGS BY:
Yolyanko el Habanero.

Contents

4   Meet the Rottweiler

12   Description of the Rottweiler

20   Are You a Rottie Person?

26   Selecting a Breeder

30   Finding the Right Puppy

38   Welcoming the Rottweiler

46   House-training Your Rottie

50   Rottweiler Puppy Training

60   Home Care for Your Rottie

68   Feeding Your Rottweiler

72   Grooming Your Rottweiler

76   Keeping Your Rottie Active

84   Your Rottie and His Vet

94   Your Aging Rottweiler

Meet the Rottweiler

T he Rottweiler is a handsome, strong, intelligent and protective dog. He ranks high in popularity in the United States among the breeds recognized by the American Kennel Club (AKC) and he is a favorite of many dog enthusiasts. However, the Rottweiler is not the breed for everyone. Before purchasing this breed, you should do some research and make inquiries of responsible breeders. The history of the Rottweiler, like the history of many other breeds, is

The breed was often used for cart-pulling duties. Today the Rottweiler participates in carting more for fun and for the amusement of his young friends.

complicated, and much of it is open to speculation. What is known is that the breed comes down from the Mastiff-type dogs of the Romans in the time of Julius Caesar. These were dogs that were intelligent and tough, and they were willing workers that could drive cattle as well as guard their masters. When the Roman army decided that the troops should be fed fresh meat, the dogs became part of the army, traveling with the troops, guarding and herding the cattle that would become the soldiers' meals.

The police and military have used Rottweilers for many search-and-rescue operations.

About 74 AD, one particular military campaign crossed the Alps and settled in what is now southern Germany, bringing their dogs with them. Agriculture and cattle remained the primary occupations of this area, regardless of which army or government was in control. The dogs continued to be a necessary part of the work day, taking the cattle to market. A Christian church was

The Rottweiler is capable of acting as an assistance dog, aiding the wheelchair-bound in their everyday tasks.

built on the site of the former Roman baths in about 700 AD. As the excavation took place, red tiles were found and the site was thus named *das Rote Wil* (the red tile), which eventually became the town of Rottweil, from which the Rottweiler was named.

The breed was highly prized in the city, not only to drive the cattle to market but also to protect households and inhabitants. In addition to their herding abilities, the dogs were found to be fearless in hunting bear and boar as well as capable of pulling the milk and meat carts. This was, indeed, a breed that served many purposes. A well-known story tells of the butcher, after drinking on a Saturday afternoon when his shop had closed, who would tie his bag of coins around the dog's neck to safeguard the money on the perhaps wobbly walk home.

The town of Rottweil became a trading center, and the cattle continued to play a prominent part of its history. Butchers settled in the area and more dogs were needed to take the cattle to market; this continued until around 1840. At that time, driving cattle to market was outlawed and the railroad soon took the job of moving cattle away from the dogs. The breed declined and, by 1882, one poor specimen of Rottweiler represented the breed at a dog show in Heilbronn, Germany. However, by 1901 a combined dog club for the Rottweiler and Leonberger was formed and the Rottweiler received a brief reprieve from obscurity. The club did not exist for long but, during this period, the first standard for the breed was drawn up.

By 1907, the Deutscher Rottweiler Klub was formed. In April of the same year, a second club, the International Rottweiler Klub, was also

Every new generation of Rottweiler should retain the breed's prized characteristics. This promising puppy already glistens with the breed's nobility and confidence.

Rottweiler

Rottweilers are strong, muscular, intelligent, striking in looks and ever-alert to what's going on around them.

formed. To make for more confusion among the Rottweiler breeders, a third club, the South German Rottweiler Club, was started in 1919. By 1921, the three clubs decided to work together for the betterment of

3,400 Rottweilers were listed in the first combined registry of the three clubs.

After World War I, as Germans began to emigrate to the United States, they brought their dogs with them. The first Rottweiler was

The Rottweiler presents an easily recognizable profile, with impressive size and musculature. Although breed standards vary slightly from country to country, breeders around the world strive to keep the Rottweiler true to type.

the breed, and by 1924 all three clubs had merged into one club, the Allgemeiner Deutscher Rottweiler Klub (ADRK). The breed had regained popularity and

admitted to the AKC stud book in 1931 and the breed began to enjoy some popularity stateside. After World War II, American soldiers returned to the States with memories of the German dog that could do a day's work guarding the troops as well as the supplies, and the breed continued to gain support among Americans. The standard was accepted by the American Kennel Club in 1935, and the first American Rottweiler gained his show championship in 1948. However, one of the breed earned his obedience championship in 1939. The American Rottweiler Club was formed in 1971 and the first national specialty show for the breed was held in 1981.

The breed remained low in popularity in America through the 1970s, but by the 1980s, with an increased need for home security, the Rottweiler began its upward climb in popularity. The Rottweiler enjoyed a few years in the 1990s as the

Sleeve training is a component of police-dog training as well as Schutzhund work, a traditional German training discipline for protection dogs. This type of training should only be done by a professional.

second most popular breed in America. Today the breed struggles with its reputation as cities try to pass legislation against breeds including the American Pit Bull Terrier, the Staffordshire Terrier, the Doberman Pinscher and the Rottweiler. For these reasons, if you are considering bringing a Rottweiler into your household, you should check with local ordinances to make certain that there is no breed-specific legislation against the Rottweiler. Even some homeowners' insurances policies have bans on certain breeds.

Although some people have a negative opinion of the breed, well-bred Rottweilers are temperamentally sound, multi-talented dogs. Breeders ensure that only the best qualities are passed to each generation.

MEET THE ROTTWEILER

Overview

- Ancestors of the Rottie were workers of the ancient Romans, guarding, driving and herding their cattle and serving at other tasks.
- The Rottweiler was named after Rottweil, the German city to which its establishment can be traced.
- As the need for the breed as a worker diminished, so did the Rottweiler's popularity.
- German breed clubs saved the breed from extinction, allowing it to flourish and capture the attention of fanciers outside Germany. American soldiers were especially impressed by these working dogs, which they had seen during both World Wars.

CHAPTER 2

Description of the Rottweiler

Every breed of dog registered with the American Kennel Club (AKC) has an official standard, a written description that gives a mental picture of how the breed should look, move and act. The Rottweiler is a working breed and is classified in the AKC's Working Group. Even though it has strong herding abilities, it is not officially considered to be a herding dog. Working dogs like the Rottie are known for their abilities to guard and protect, to pull a cart or a sled or to rescue drowning people. These are dogs who, many for centuries as with

The guard duties of most Rottweilers today revolve around protecting his home and family.

the Rottweiler, have been used by man to assist him in his work.

The Rottweiler is a fairly large and robust dog, black in color with rust markings. He is a powerful dog with a compact and substantial build. Dogs are to be between 24 and 27 inches high at the shoulders; bitches are slightly smaller but still show the substantial build of the male. The breed is slightly longer than tall and should give a powerful appearance. The standard notes that the Rottie should look alert, noble and self-assured.

Obviously, strength and muscle are highly desirable in the breed. The standard states that the neck is powerful and well muscled; the chest is roomy, broad and deep. The legs are strongly developed with heavy bone and the hindquarters are very broad and well muscled. He should have a straight, dense and coarse outer coat and he is shown in a

Although classified and known primarily as a working breed, the Rottweiler is a skilled herding dog and is eligible to compete in American Kennel Club herding tests and trials.

The Rottie's coat is sleek black, with well-defined rust-colored markings over the eyes, on the cheeks, muzzle and throat, on the chest and legs, under the tail and on the toes.

The Rottweiler is selective in choosing his friends, but once you've earned his loyalty, you've gained a devoted friend for life.

natural state with no trimming of the coat.

His gait is described as that of a trotter and "his movement should be balanced, harmonious, sure, powerful and unhindered with strong forereach and a powerful rear drive. The motion is effortless, efficient and ground-covering."

The standard states, "The Rottweiler is basically a calm, confident and courageous dog with a self-assured aloofness that does not lend itself to immediate and indiscriminate friend-

The Rottweiler is described as moving like a "trotter." He is capable of speed and covers much ground, propelled by muscular fore- and hindquarters.

ships. The Rottweiler is self-confident and responds quietly and with a wait-and-see attitude to influences in his environment. He has an inherent desire to protect

Skull: Cranium.

Stop: Indentation between the eyes at point of nasal bones and skull.

Muzzle: Foreface or region of head in front of eyes.

Lip: Fleshy portion of upper and lower jaws.

Flews: Hanging part of upper lip.

Withers: Highest part of the back, at the base of neck above the shoulders.

Shoulder: Upper point of forequarters; the region of the two shoulder blades.

Chest: Thoracic cavity (enclosed by ribs).

Forechest: Sternum.

Forequarters: Front assembly from shoulder to feet.

Upper arm: Region between shoulder blade and forearm.

Elbow: Region where forearm and arm meet.

Forearm: Region between arm and wrist.

Dewclaw: Extra digit on inside of leg; fifth toe.

Carpus: Wrist.

Occiput: Upper back part of skull; apex.

Topline: Outline from withers to tailset.

Brisket: Lower chest.

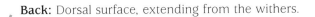

Back: Dorsal surface, extending from the withers.

Loin: Lumbar region between ribs and pelvis.

Body: Region between the fore- and hindquarters.

Croup: Pelvic region; rump.

Stern: Tail.

Hip: Joint of pelvis and upper thigh bone.

Hindquarters: Rear assembly from pelvis to feet.

Upper thigh: Region from hip joint to stifle.

Stifle: Knee.

Lower thigh: Hindquarter region from stifle to hock; second thigh.

Flank: Region between last rib and hip.

Hock: Tarsus or heel.

Pastern: Region between wrist and toes.

Abdomen: Surface beneath the chest and hindquarters; belly.

Digit: Toe.

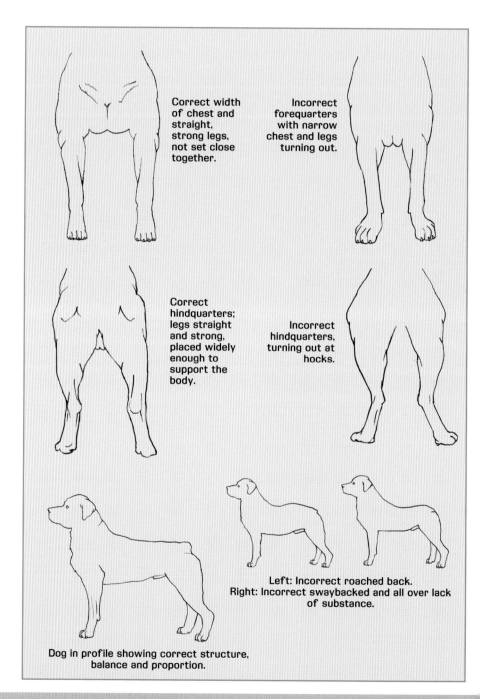

Correct width of chest and straight, strong legs, not set close together.

Incorrect forequarters with narrow chest and legs turning out.

Correct hindquarters; legs straight and strong, placed widely enough to support the body.

Incorrect hindquarters, turning out at hocks.

Left: Incorrect roached back.
Right: Incorrect swaybacked and all over lack of substance.

Dog in profile showing correct structure, balance and proportion.

home and family, and is an intelligent dog of extreme hardness and adaptability with a strong willingness to work, making him especially suited as a companion, guardian and general all-purpose dog."

There are many reasons why one would want to own this breed! A well-bred Rottweiler can be a joy to have as a pet. He can be an extremely affectionate companion and he is very trainable with his high degree of intelligence. However, the prospective Rottweiler owner must realize that this is not the right breed for everyone. The dog must be trained at an early age and must understand what is acceptable behavior and what is not. In addition, he must know that unacceptable behavior will not be tolerated. He must understand that you are the leader in the household and that he will not get his way by being a bully. Early training in obedience is one of the easiest ways to establish who is in control.

DESCRIPTION OF THE ROTTWEILER

Overview

- A breed standard is an official document, set forth by the parent club and approved by the AKC, which describes the Rottweiler's ideal physical conformation, character and movement.
- The Rottie's body should be muscular with a deep, broad chest and well-developed legs.
- The Rottie's temperament is one of confidence. He selects his friends carefully and becomes very loyal to and protective of those close to him.
- The Rottweiler has a short double coat, black in color with rich markings of rust to mahogany.

Are You a Rottie Person?

Before purchasing your Rottweiler, you must give some thought to the personality and characteristics of this breed to determine if this is the breed for you. This is not a dog for the laid-back owner who will not give the dog the training and attention that he deserves. In addition, this is not always a dog for the first-time puppy owner. This is a dog for the individual who has studied up on the breed, understands its characteristics and is willing to train the dog and give him the time that he will need.

The best owner for a Rottie is an active person who enjoys the outdoors and participating in a range of activities with his dog.

You should answer the following questions before purchasing a Rottweiler:

1. Do you have the time to give to a dog? He will need care, companionship, training and grooming. This is almost like having a child, except the dog remains a child and will always require your care.

2. Do you have a fenced-in yard for your Rottweiler? This is not a breed that you can leave tied out on the porch or let loose. He must have a secure area in which to run and exercise.

3. Have you owned a dog previously and did that dog live a long and happy life with your family?

4. Have you checked with your local offices to make certain that there are no breed-specific laws in your town or neighborhood? Some communities will not allow certain breeds of dog, and the Rottweiler may be one of them.

Although an energetic dog that needs plenty of outdoor exercise, the Rottie also needs time spent in the home with his owners. He wants to be a true part of the family.

Rottweilers can be big teddy bears around the children in their lives! Of course, dogs and children always must be introduced carefully, supervised in their interactions and know how to treat each other with respect.

5. Understand that your neighbors may not be pleased with your bringing this breed into the neighborhood. Have you spoken to them about your plans?

6. Even if the Rottweiler requires a minimum of grooming, your dog will require some care. Do you have the time to do this?

Let's take each question one at a time:

1. Do you have the time to give to a dog? Having time for a dog does not mean that you cannot work and own a dog. Your pet will need quality time, though, just as a child does. He must be fed two times a day and exercised several times a day. He needs to be petted and loved, and he will like to go for rides in the car with you. You must work with him to have an obedient dog who has good manners. Your dog should have at least two good outings a day, and that means a walk or a good romp in the morning and the evening. Never let him out loose to run the neighborhood.

2. Do you have a fenced-in yard? Your yard should be large enough to allow you to throw a ball and for your dog to run with it. Remember, it is your responsibility to keep the yard clean of feces. When walking your dog it is essential to carry a plastic bag or two to pick up droppings. These can be easily dropped in a trash receptacle on your way home.

3. Have you owned a dog previously? This will give you a good idea of what a dog expects from you and what you must do for your dog. Since the Rottweiler is one of the

strongest dogs in the canine world, you must be able to handle him. In addition, the Rottweiler is smart and needs an owner who is equally as your area. Your local council may not allow certain breeds in the area and the Rottweiler just may be one of these breeds.

The Rottweiler owner must have control of the dog at all times. Walks in public places must always be on lead, although the dog will appreciate time for free running in securely fenced areas.

smart as, or smarter than, he is!

4. Be sure to check with your local offices and find out if there are any breed-specific laws for

5. You should talk to your neighbors about adding a Rottweiler to your household. Give them some information on the breed and reassure them

that you are purchasing your puppy from a responsible breeder and that you will give this dog the time, the care and the training that he will need.

6. Grooming is minimal with

Flying high! Although he has considerable mass, the Rottweiler is agile. This, coupled with his intelligence and trainability, makes him capable of achieving success at high levels of obedience. This Rottie completes the retrieve over the high jump, an advanced exercise.

this breed, but you will need to trim his toenails, wash his face once or twice a week, keep his ears clean and give him baths as needed.

Good humor and a childlike sense of adventure are required for owning a Rottweiler, as these are traits that the breed embraces. You also must be physically fit and enjoy activity, also characteristics that the

Rottweiler appreciates. Experience with dogs and a well-grounded sense of responsibility are keys to owning this large and powerful dog, a dog that demands respect and under-standing. Being able to train the Rottweiler, physically and mentally, is of paramount importance as well.

In spite of the toughness of the dog and the occasional difficulty in acceptance of the breed by one's neighbors, the Rottweiler is appreciated for his intelligence, his devotion to his family, his abilities for guarding those around him and their possessions and his good looks. However, do learn about the breed before rushing out and buying the first puppy you see.

For more information about the Rottweiler, go to your local library and check out any other books on the breed. In addition, an excellent source of information can be found on the Internet at the American Rottweiler Club (ARC) website: www.amrottclub. org. This website is an excellent source of information on the breed as well as a directory of local Rottweiler clubs and contact people.

ARE YOU A ROTTIE PERSON?

Overview

- The Rottweiler person is ready and able to assume a position of authority with his intelligent, strong dog.
- The Rottweiler person has time to spend with his dog, as well as ample space to give the dog the exercise he needs.
- The Rottie person makes sure that his new dog will be welcome in the community.
- The Rottweiler person is ready to train his dog to become a reliable, well-mannered canine citizen.

Selecting a Breeder

When you buy your Rottweiler, you will want to buy a healthy puppy from a responsible breeder. A responsible breeder is someone who has given considerable thought before breeding his bitch. He considers health problems in the breed, has room in his home or kennel for a litter of puppies and has the time to give to a litter. He does not breed to the dog down the block because it is easy and because he wants his children to experience the miracle of birth.

A good breeder is a member of the breed club and participates with her dogs in shows and other club events.

A responsible breeder is someone who is dedicated to the breed and to breeding out any faults and hereditary problems, and whose overall interest is in improving the breed. He will study pedigrees and see what the leading stud dogs are producing. To find the right stud dog for his bitch, he may fly the bitch across the country to breed to a particular stud dog, or he may drive the bitch to a dog located many miles away. He may have only one or two litters per year, which means that there may not be a puppy ready for you when you first make your inquiries. Remember that you are purchasing a new family member and usually the wait will be well worthwhile.

Check out the AKC's website at www.amrottclub.com for a listing of local Rottweiler clubs. You should be able to find one in your area, or at least in your state, as there are many clubs dedicated to the breed. The local

Observe the Rotties being shown at a dog show. After their turn in the ring, introduce yourself to some handlers and express your interest in the breed. This is a wonderful way to make contacts and get breeder referrals.

Look for a breeder with a loving attitude toward all of the puppies. She provides the litter with essential early socialization by handling them, petting them and introducing them to the world outside the whelping box.

club should be able to direct you to a responsible breeder and should be able to answer any questions that you may have.

The responsible Rottweiler breeder will probably be someone who has been breeding for some years and someone who is known on the national level. He will be a member of the local Rottweiler club and will also belong to the American Rottweiler Club.

The responsible breeder will show you his kennel, if he has one, or invite you into his home to see the puppies. The areas will be clean and smell good. The breeder will show you the dam of the puppy that you are looking at and she will be clean, will smell good and will be groomed. The puppies will also be clean, with trimmed toenails and clean faces. The breeder may show you only one or two puppies, as he may not show you the puppies that are already sold

Among the questions the breeder will ask you are if you have ample space for a Rottweiler, if you have a fenced yard and if you have other pets. This Rottie seems quite content among his pack of canine housemates.

or that he is going to keep.

The breeder will also have questions for you. Have you owned a dog before? How many have you had and have you ever owned a Rottweiler? Did your dogs live long lives? Do you have a fenced yard? How many children do you have and what are their ages? Are you willing to spend time teaching your children how to treat the new family member? Have you ever done any dog training and are you willing to go to obedience classes with your dog? Are there any other pets in your household? Do

not be offended by these questions. The breeder has invested a lot of effort, time and money into the litter and his first priority is to place each pup in a caring and appropriate household where the pup will be wanted, loved and cared for properly.

Rough-and-tumble play with older dogs teaches the pup that seniority rules in the dog pack. The pup learns important lessons by discovering just how far he can push his playmate's limits.

SELECTING A BREEDER

Overview

- Finding a reputable breeder is a prospective owner's obligation. Contact the AKC or the American Rottweiler Club to be referred to ethical breeders.
- Know what to expect from a quality breeder and keep looking until you find someone with whom you are completely comfortable.
- Take a look around the breeder's premises and be prepared with your list of questions. Likewise, be prepared to answer the questions that the breeder has for you.

Finding the Right Puppy

Y ou are now ready to select your puppy. You have decided that you are a Rottweiler person and that you can live with this very game, large, courageous and smart dog. You have checked out the local ordinances for breed-specific legislation and you have talked to your neighbors about bringing a Rottweiler into the community. Your entire family is ready for this new arrival into your home and lives. You have done your homework on the breed and have located a responsible breeder who has a litter available.

Breeders keep puppies until at least eight weeks of age. After that time will come the day when each pup will kiss Mom goodbye and go home with a new family.

You arrive at the appointed time and the breeder has the Rottweiler puppies ready for you to look at. They should be a happy bunch, clean and groomed. Their noses will be wet, their coats will have a glow or sheen and they will have a nice covering of flesh over their ribs. You will be ready to pick up one of these rascals and cuddle him in your arms.

Although it will be difficult, don't lose your heart to the first puppy you see. Take time to get to know each pup in the litter and see which one appeals to you most; the breeder's advice will also be invaluable in finding the perfect match.

You should ask the breeder if the sire and dam of the litter have had their temperaments tested. These tests are offered by the American Temperament Test Society (ATTS). Responsible breeders will be familiar with this organization and will have had their animals tested. The breeder will show you the score sheet and you can easily determine if the parents are temperamentally sound. In addition, this is an excellent indication that this is a responsible Rottweiler breeder.

Temperament testing by the ATTS

At least the dam of the litter should be with the breeder; be sure to meet her. Don't be shy about asking to see documentation of the parents' health clearances and temperament testing, if the latter has been done.

is done on dogs that are at least 18 months of age; therefore puppies are not tested, but the sire and dam of a litter can be tested. The test is like a simulated walk through a park or a neighborhood where everyday situations are encountered. Neutral, friendly and threatening situations are encountered to see what the dog's reactions are to the various stimuli. Problems that are looked for are unprovoked aggression, panic without recovery and strong avoidance. Behavior toward strangers, reaction to auditory, visual and tactile stimuli and self-protective and aggressive behavior are also observed. The dog is on a loose lead for the test, which takes about ten minutes to complete. As of December, 2002, the ATTS had tested 4,311 Rottweilers, of which 3,539 passed, giving an 82.1% passing rate, which is a high rate compared to some other breeds.

Some breeders will have the temperaments of their puppies tested by a professional, their veterinarian or another dog breeder. They will find the high-energy pup and the pup that is slower in responding. They will find the pup with the independent spirit and the one that wants to follow the pack. If the litter has been tested, the breeder will suggest which pup he thinks will be best for your family. If the litter has not been tested, you can do a few simple tests while you are sitting on the floor playing with the pups.

Pat your leg or snap your finger and see which pup comes up to you first. Clap your hands and see if any puppy shies away from you. See how the pups play with one another. Watch for the one that has the personality that most appeals to you, as

Your entire family should play a part in the puppy selection, so bring them along to make sure everyone agrees on the new addition to the family.

CHAPTER 5

Part of the "fun" of puppy ownership is dealing with puppy teeth! Your teething pup will be a voracious chewer and will need safe, strong toys to soothe his aching gums and direct his chewing energies properly.

this will probably be the puppy that you will take home. Look for the puppy that appears to be "in the middle," not overly rambunctious, aggressive or submissive. You want the happy pup, not the wild one. Spend some time selecting your puppy and, if you are hesitant, tell the breeder that you would like to go home and think it over. This is a major decision, as you are adding a family member who may be with you for 10 to 12 years, or even more. Be sure to get the puppy that you will all be happy with.

Have you given much thought to the sex of your puppy? Do you prefer a male or a female? Which one is right for you? Both sexes are loving and loyal, and the differences are due more to individual personalities than to sex. The Rottweiler female can be a bit more moody, depending on her whims and hormonal peaks, but is generally easy to live with and a sweet companion. The male bonds closely to his master and family and is a significantly larger animal, often 2 inches or more taller than the female. Both animals are fairly large and powerful.

Although males tend to be more even-tempered than bitches, they are also more physical and exuberant during adolescence, which can be problematic in a strong and powerful dog. An untrained male also can become dominant with people and other dogs. A solid foundation in obedience is necessary if you want the dog to respect you as his (or her) leader. Unneutered males tend to be more territorial, especially with other male dogs, though both male and female Rotts are protective of home and family.

Since you will likely be neutering or spaying your pet Rottweiler, most of the sexually related problems that "whole" dogs encounter will not be factors. If you are considering a Rottweiler for showing, then you will have to contend with the bitch's twice-annual estrus (heat cycle) and the male's year-round search for a willing female in heat. Male Rottweilers, like males of other species, are far more interested in reproduction than are females. Males will mount females or whoever passes by at the right moment, tend to mark their territory with small amounts of urine (although no amount of urine is that small inside your home) and will wander off in search of a partner (ah, wanderlust!).

A trio of happy, outgoing littermates, enjoying some sunshine.

Aside from the behavioral benefits of neutering and spaying, sexually altered dogs of both sexes are protected from or enjoy less risk of many health problems, including repro-ductive cancers.

Check your chosen puppy's bite. The bite will change slightly as the pup's bones develop, but the breeder should be able to predict that the bite will mature correctly.

Once you have decided on the most suitable puppy from the litter, an outgoing, happy boy or girl who shows all indications of good health, proper social-ization and Rottweiler confi-dence and charm, you are on your way to bringing your new acquisition into your household. The excitement is just about to start, and there's nothing to compare to the arrival of a Rottweiler baby.

FINDING THE RIGHT PUPPY

Overview

- Visit the litter to see the puppies firsthand. You are seeking sound puppies with all indications of being in good health.
- Don't be swept away by the first puppy you see. Get to know each pup and take the time to determine which, if any, is right for you.
- Ask if the parents of the litter have been temperament tested.
- Trust your breeder to recommend a puppy that fits your lifestyle and personality.
- Consider the differences between males and females in the breed to decide which sex you'd prefer to live with.

Welcoming the Rottweiler

A new Rottweiler puppy in your home brings much excitement and joy along with many responsibilities. Before welcoming your pup into your home, there are some essentials that you will need. First, you should buy food and water bowls and a leash and collar. You should also purchase a crate for your puppy. He will not only sleep in his crate but also spend his time there anytime he is home alone. In very short order, your puppy will learn that the crate is his second "home," and he will feel

Puppies need much time to rest, so don't be surprised if your young Rottie's explorations of his new surroundings are interspersed with frequent naps.

safe and secure when he is in his crate. When the pup is left uncrated and alone, he will quickly become bored and begin to chew on the furniture, the woodwork and anything else within reach. Keeping him in a confined area when you are away will eliminate these problems. Be sure to line the crate with several towels or a washable blanket so that your puppy will be comfortable.

One thing you can be sure of— your puppy will be curious about everything and won't be shy about investigating.

If you are driving some distance to pick up your pet, take along a towel or two, some water and your leash and collar. Also take along some plastic baggies and a roll of paper towels in case there are any potty accidents along the way.

A SAFE HOME IS A HAPPY HOME

Before bringing your puppy into the house, you should be aware that a small puppy can be like a toddler and there are dangers in the household that must be eliminated. Electrical

Inspect your home inside and out, and be sure that there is nothing dangerous in any areas to which your inquisitive pup has access.

wires should be raised off the floor and hidden from view, as they are very tempting as chewable objects. Swimming pools can be very dangerous, so make certain that your puppy can't get into, or fall into, the pool. Some barricades will be necessary to prevent an accident. Not all dogs can swim, and those with short legs or heavy bodies cannot climb out of the pool. Watch your deck railings and make sure that your puppy cannot slip through the openings and fall.

If you have young children in the house, you must see that they understand that the small puppy is a living being that must be treated gently. They cannot ride on him or pull his ears, and he cannot be picked up carelessly and dropped. This is your responsibility. A child who is taught about animals at an early age can become a lifelong compassionate animal lover and owner.

Use your common sense! Consider where a young child can get into trouble, and your puppy will be right behind him! When he comes into the house for the first time (after he has relieved himself outside), let him investigate his new home and surroundings,] and give him a light meal and some water. When he is tired, take him outside again for a potty trip and then tuck him into his crate, either to take a nap or, hopefully, to sleep through the night.

The first day or two for your puppy should be fairly quiet. This will give him time to get used to his new home, surroundings and family members. He may cry a bit during the first night,but if you put a puppy toy or a soft, woolly sweater in his crate, it will give him some warmth and security. A nearby ticking clock or a radio playing soft music can also be helpful. Remember, he has been uprooted from a sibling or two, his mother, and his familiar breeder, and he will need a day or two to get used to his new family. If he should cry during the first night, let him be and he will eventually quiet down and sleep. By the third night, he should be well settled in. Have patience and, within a week or less, it will seem to you, your family and the puppy that you have all been together for years.

SOCIALIZATION

This actually puppy-proofs your puppy, not your house. Puppy socialization is your Rottweiler's insurance policy to happy, stable adulthood and is, without question, the most important element in a Rottweiler puppy's intro-

duction to the human world. Rotties are, by nature, gregarious with people and other dogs and are rarely aggressive or suspicious of strangers. However, it has been proven that unsocialized pups grow up to be spooky, insecure, and fearful of people, children

The breeder will provide you with details of your pup's feeding and advise you about how to continue. Have some food and bowls on hand for your puppy.

and strange places. Many turn into fear biters or become aggressive with other dogs, strangers, even family members. Such dogs can seldom be rehabilitated and often end up abandoned in animal shelters where they are likely eventually euthanized. Puppy socialization lays the foundation for a well-behaved adult canine, thus

the puppy's first 20 weeks of life. Once he leaves the safety of his mom and litter-mates at eight to ten weeks of age, your job begins. Start with a quiet, uncomplicated household for the first day or two, then gradually

Children in the home should spend supervised time with your puppy, engaging him in play with his toys. Fun time spent together helps build the dog-owner bond while keeping him active.

preventing those behaviors that lead to abandonment and, unfortunately, euthanasia.

The primary social-ization period occurs during

introduce him to the sights and sounds of his new human world. Frequent interaction with children, new people and other dogs is essential at this age. Visit new places (dog-friendly, of course) like parks or even the local strip mall where there are crowds of people. (Be sure you're not going into places that do not allow dogs, as meeting a nasty security guard or police officer will not be a good socialization experience for your black-and-tan baby.) Set a goal of two new places a week for the next two months. Keep these new situations upbeat and positive, which will create a positive attitude toward future encounters.

"Positive" is especially important when visiting your veterinarian. You don't want a pup that quakes with fear every time he sets a paw inside his doctor's office. Make sure your vet is a dog lover as well as a dog doctor.

Your puppy also will need supervised exposure to children. Rotties are generally good with young-

sters, but both dog and child must learn how to behave properly with each other. Puppies of all breeds tend to view little people as litter-mates and will exert the upper paw (a dominance ploy) over the child. Children must be taught how to properly play with

Your pup will benefit from meeting other canine youngsters. This Rottie has a new friend in a Shiba puppy.

the dog and to respect his privacy. Likewise, adult family members should supervise and teach the puppy not to nip or jump up on the kids. A Rottweiler who has bad experiences with children can set up a dangerous situation for all involved. Socializing the Rottie to like kids, especially if your dog is going to have youngsters around him on a regular basis, couldn't be more important. Even if you don't have children of your own, keep in mind that neighbors, family members and other visitors may bring their children into your home or yard.

Take your Rottweiler

Your Rottie's wardrobe must include an everyday collar to which his ID tags are attached. This is important throughout his life.

Your Rottweiler's crate has many uses: house-breaking, safety and traveling, to name a few. The crate you purchase for your puppy should be large enough to house a fully grown Rottweiler.

youngster to puppy school. Some classes accept pups from 10 to 12 weeks of age, with one series of puppy shots as a health require-ment. The younger the pup, the easier it is to shape good behavior patterns. A good puppy class teaches proper canine social etiquette rather than rigid obedience skills. Your puppy will meet and play with young dogs of other breeds and you will learn about the positive teaching tools you'll need to train your pup. Puppy class is important for both novice and experienced puppy folks. If you're a smart Rottweiler owner, you won't stop there and will continue on with a basic obedience class. Of course, you want the best-behaved Rottweiler in the neighborhood!

Remember this: there is a direct correlation between the quality and amount of time you spend with your puppy during his first 20 weeks of life and the character of the adult dog he will become. You cannot recapture this valuable learning period, so make the most of it.

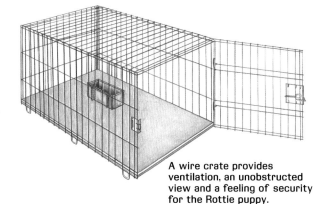

A wire crate provides ventilation, an unobstructed view and a feeling of security for the Rottie puppy.

WELCOMING THE ROTTWEILER

Overview

- Go to the pet store to stock up on the puppy basics. Puppy food, bowls, a collar and ID tags, toys, a leash, a crate and a brush are among the items you will need to have on hand.
- Make your home safe for your puppy by removing potential dangers from the dog's environment indoors and out.
- Introduce your pup to children, other dogs and new situations. Keep new experiences positive and fun and he will grow up well socialized and well adjusted.
- A puppy class is a great way to socialize and train your new pup.

House-training Your Rottie

Your dog must be housebroken, and this task should begin as soon as you bring him home. Diligence during the first two or three weeks will surely pay off, and this should be a relatively easy job since the Rottweiler is so smart. Every time your puppy wakes up from a nap, he should be quickly taken outside. Watch him and praise him with "Good boy!" when he urinates or defecates, then give him a pat on the head and take him inside. He may have a few accidents, but with the appropriate "No" from you he will

You must housebreak your Rottweiler puppy by training him to relieve himself outdoors. Start taking him out for toileting as soon as you get him home.

quickly learn that it is better to go outside and do his "job" than to do it on the kitchen floor and be scolded.

You will soon learn the habits of your dog. However, at the following times it is essential to take your puppy out: when he gets up in the morning, after he eats, before he goes to bed and after long naps. As he matures, most dogs will only have to go out three or four times a day. Some dogs will go to the door and bark when they want to be let out and others will nervously circle around. Watch and learn from his signs. Of course, crates are a major help in housebreaking, as most dogs will not want to dirty their living quarters.

Just be patient with the house-breaking, as this can sometimes be a trying time. It is simply essential to have a clean house dog. Life will be much easier for all of you—not to mention much better for the carpeting!

Get an adult-sized large crate from the outset. Keep in mind the Rottie's eventual size of up to 27 inches tall at the shoulder, and purchase a crate that will allow him to sit, stand and stretch out comfortably at full size.

Some breeders take the time to introduce their pups to crates before they leave for new homes, making crate-training a little easier for new owners.

Who is going to take the driver's seat in your relationship with your Rottweiler? Your Rottie will if you let him, though that's not the way to raise a dog with whom you can live happily.

Never (that is spelled N-E-V-E-R) rub your puppy's nose in his mistake or strike your puppy or adult dog with your hand, a newspaper or other object to correct him. He will not understand and will only become fearful of the person who is hitting him.

Potty hint: remove puppy's water after 7 p.m. to aid in nighttime bladder control. If he gets thirsty, offer him an ice cube. Then just watch him race for the refrigerator when he hears the rattle of the ice cube tray.

Despite its many benefits, crate use can be abused.

Puppies under 12 weeks of age should never be confined for more than two hours at a time unless, of course, they are sleeping. A general rule of thumb is three hours maximum for a three-month old pup, four or five for the four- to five-month old, and no more than six hours for dogs over six months of age. If you're unable to be home to release the dog, arrange for a relative, neighbor or dog-sitter to let him out to exercise and potty.

Keep in mind while training: use your common sense, be consistent and have patience.

HOUSE-TRAINING YOUR ROTTIE

Overview

- The first hurdle for all puppy owners is housebreaking, teaching the dog clean toileting habits.
- Never punish your Rottie for accidents. Don't even scold him unless you catch him in the act.
- Remove puppy's water after 7 p.m. to aid in nighttime bladder control.
- The crate is the best answer to house-training your Rottweiler. Learn how to use a crate, not abuse it.

Rottweiler Puppy Training

Your puppy should be well socialized when you bring him home. He will be used to family and strangers, and average noises in the house and on the street will not startle him. Socialization for your puppy is very important, and good breeders spend time socializing their litters. It is particularly helpful if there were children in the breeder's family. Let your dog meet the neighbors and play for a few minutes. Take him for short walks in public places where he will see people and other dogs as well as hear strange noises. Watch other

Accustom your puppy to a light lead and collar for his early training. As your Rottie matures, becoming larger and stronger, he will need a larger collar and accordingly stronger lead.

dogs, however, as they are not always friendly. Keep your dog on a short leash and you will have control over him so he does not jump up on anyone.

You will find it to your advantage to have a mannerly dog; therefore, some basic commands will make your dog a better canine citizen. One of the family members should attend puppy kindergarten classes with the pup, as all further training will be built on this foundation. This is a class that accepts puppies from two to five months of age. It takes about two months to complete the class. You will cover the basics: sit, heel, down and recall or come. There are definite advantages to each. Sit and heel are great helps when walking your dog. Who needs a puppy that walks between your legs, lunging forward or lagging behind, in general acting like a nut? Have your dog walking like a gentleman on your left

Training your dog means deciding on the house rules and being consistent in enforcing them. Will you allow your Rottie to become a "couch potato" or would you rather he not get up onto the furniture?

A well-trained Rottweiler knows the daily routine, such as when it's time to go for walks and to go out to relieve himself.

side and sitting as you wait to cross the street. The recall is very important if your dog either escapes from the yard or breaks his leash and you need to call him back. Remember, it is essential to have an obedient Rottweiler.

indecisive! This is not like naming a goldfish (which can change six times before the final exit). You have to use your Rottweiler's name 100 times per day! Many breeders think it wise to choose a two-syllable name,

Never under-estimate the power of socialization. A well-adjusted puppy who is comfortable around everyone will be more confident and able to learn more quickly.

Before your Rottweiler puppy comes home, you will have chosen a name for the dog. This is not a time to be

such as "Marcus" or "Lotte," so that the dog recognizes the rhythm of the name. Yes, of course, German names are best for Rottweilers! You don't want to name your proud German dog "Pedro" or "Chauncey" (though it's been done!).

In order to teach your puppy his name, you have to use it when you speak to him, always in a happy, upbeat tone. Never use the pup's name when you are correcting him, as he will associate his name with a negative experiences (and then you'll be spending thousands of dollars on doggie analysts dealing with mother-inflicted self-loathing, every psychiatrist's favorite topic). But seriously, say things like "Good, Eva, good" or "That's a handsome boy, Heinrich!" and "Good Knabe, Ludwig." Once you have achieved name recognition, you can begin teaching basic commands.

Always start your teaching exercises in a quiet, distraction-free environment. Once your pup has mastered any task, change the setting and practice in a different location like another room or outside in the yard. Next, practice with another person or a dog nearby. If the pup reacts to the new distraction

The sit command is where you will begin your Rottie's education in the basic commands.

and does not perform the exercise, take a step back with your training, make his food rewards more enticing and continue with the exercise by working without distractions for a while.

Here is a short rundown of the commands. If you attend puppy classes or obedience-training classes, you will have professional help in learning these commands. However, you and your dog can learn these very basic exercises on your own at home.

SIT COMMAND

This is the exercise with which you should begin. Place your dog on your left side as you are standing and firmly say "Sit." As you say this, run your hand down your dog's back and gently guide him into a sitting position. Praise him, hold him in this position for a few minutes, release your hand, praise him again and give him a treat. Repeat this several times a day, perhaps as many as ten times. Before long, your pup will under-stand what you want. So that all of your obedience lessons start and end on a positive note, use the sit command to begin and end every lesson.

STAY COMMAND

Teach your dog to stay in a seated position until you call him. Have your dog sit and, as you say "Stay," place your hand in front of his nose and take a step or two, no more at the beginning, away from him. After ten seconds or so, call your dog. If he gets up before the end of the command, have him sit again and repeat the stay command. When he stays until called (remembering to start with a very short period of time), praise him and give him a treat. As he learns this command, increase the space that you move away from the dog as well as the length of time that he stays.

The stay command can be used in any position and can be practiced after the sit exercise or the down exercise. Likewise, show-dog trainers use the command to

The sit/stay is accomplished by using a verbal command and your hand as a "stop" sign, indicating that the dog is to remain in the sit position.

keep the dog in a standing (or stacked) position, as this is required for the show ring.

HEEL EXERCISE

Have your dog on your left side, with his leash on, and teach him to walk with you. If your pup lunges forward, give the leash a quick snap and say a firm "No." Then continue to walk your dog, praising him as he walks nicely by your side. Again, if he lunges, snap his leash and say a smart "No." He will quickly learn that it is easier and more pleasant to walk by your side. Never allow him to lunge at someone passing by you.

You must teach your

Rotties do not like to be in submissive postures, of which the down is one. Be comforting and encouraging, using treats and praise to motivate your dog, as you ease him into the down position.

Rottweiler to heel when he is still young (and lighter). You will find it very difficult (if not impossible) to walk an untrained Rottweiler around your block (no less around the ring at a dog show). Heeling is an essential exercise for pet dogs and show dogs, and all Rottweilers must be trained to obey this most simple of exercises.

DOWN COMMAND

This will probably be the most complicated of the five basic commands to teach. Place your dog in the sit position, kneel down next to him and place your right hand under his front legs and your left hand on his shoulders. As you say "Down," gently push his front legs out into the down position. Once you have him down, talk gently to him, stroke his back so that he will be comfortable and then praise him.

All dogs must behave on lead, but this is even more important with a large dog like the Rottweiler. Walking such a strong dog will be impossible if he is allowed to pull on the lead and drag you along.

RECALL (COME) EXERCISE

Always practice the come command on-leash. You can't afford to risk failure or pup will learn that he does not have to come when called. He must learn to come reliably. Once you have pup's attention, call him from a short distance, "Puppy, come!" and give a treat when he comes to you. Gently grasp and hold his collar with one hand as you dispense the treat. This is important. You will eventually phase out the treat and switch to only hands-on praise. This maneuver also connects holding his collar with coming and treating, which will assist you in countless future behaviors. Do 10 or 12 repetitions 2 or 3 times a day. Once the pup has mastered "Come," continue to practice daily to imprint this most important behavior onto his puppy brain.

PRACTICE MAKES PERFECT

Daily obedience practice is another lifetime dog rule. Dogs will be dogs, and, if we don't maintain their skills, they will sink back into sloppy, inattentive behaviors that will be harder to correct. Incorporate these basic commands into your daily routine, and your dog will remain a gentleman of whom you can be proud.

Keep sessions short, no longer than ten minutes at first, so your puppy won't get bored or lose his enthusiasm. In time, he will be able to concentrate for longer

When your Rottie hears you call him, he should drop whatever he is doing and get ready to find you.

periods. Watch for signs of boredom and loss of attention. Vary the exercises to keep his enthusiasm level high. Always keep your training sessions positive and upbeat. Use lots of praise, praise and more praise! Never train your dog or puppy if you are in a grumpy mood. You will lose patience and he will think it is his fault. That will reverse any progress the two of you have made.

A big part of training is patience, persistence and routine. Teach each command the same way every time. Do not lose your patience with the dog, as he will not understand what you are doing, and reward him for doing his command properly. With a Rottweiler, you will find that your puppy will learn these commands very quickly. Your friends, when they come to your house for a dinner party, will also appreciate a well-behaved dog who will not jump up on them or land in their laps while they are having cocktails.

ROTTWEILER PUPPY TRAINING

Overview

- A puppy class takes advantage of your Rottie's aptitude to learn at a young age while exposing him to other people and dogs and teaching you how to teach your dog.
- Pick a name for your pup and use it! Name recognition is important in training.
- The basic commands include come, sit, stay, down and heel.
- Practice with your Rottweiler daily so that he becomes consistent 100% of the time. His reliability in the basic commands is essential for both good manners and his safety.

Home Care for Your Rottie

CHAPTER 9

E very home with a pet should have a first-aid kit. You can acquire all required items at one time but more likely you will add them to your kit (oftentimes a box) as you need them. Here are the items you will need:

- Alcohol for cleaning a wound;
- Antibiotic salve for treating the wound;
- Over-the-counter eye wash in case your dog gets something in his eyes or just needs to have his eyes cleaned— "to get the red out";
- Forceps for pulling out wood ticks, thorns and burs;
- Styptic powder for when a toenail

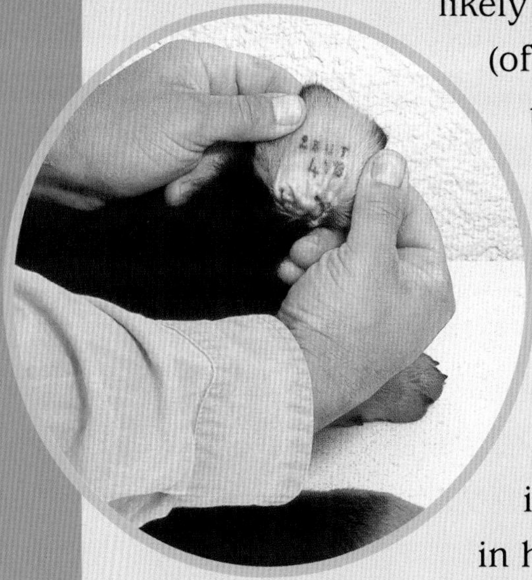

Proper identification is a must. Along with the traditional collar and ID tags, consider a permanent form of ID such as tattooing, shown here on the pup's ear flap, or microchipping.

has been trimmed too short and bleeds;

- Rectal thermometer;
- A nylon stocking to be used as a muzzle if your pet should be badly injured.

Your Rottie may take time to smell the flowers, and hopefully he won't encounter any insects that don't appreciate his trespassing! Know how to deal with first-aid situations like bee stings and insect bites.

Many of these items can be purchased very reasonably from your local drug store.

Once your dog is full-grown and remaining in good health, he will only need a yearly visit to the veterinary clinic for a checkup and a booster shot for the vaccines. At these visits, the veterinarian will probably give your Rottie's teeth an examination and possible scraping. You also may purchase a dental tool and clean the teeth yourself. Set the dog on the grooming table with his head secured and gently scrape away any tartar. Some animals will let you do this and others will not. A crunchy dog treat every night before bedtime will help to keep the tartar down.

Your pup's baby teeth eventually will be replaced with his permanent teeth. During teething, check his mouth regularly to see that teeth are falling out and coming in as they should.

Your vet may also empty the dog's anal sacs if needed. Expressing the anal glands is not a very pleasurable task, besides being quite smelly, and you may find that it is easier to have this done during the yearly trip to the clinic. On occasion the anal glands will become impacted, which will require surgery to clean them out.

By now you know your dog well; you know how much he eats and sleeps and how hard he plays. As with all of us, on occasion he may "go off his feed" or appear to be sick. If he has been nauseated for 24 to 36 hours, has had diarrhea for the same amount of time or has been drinking excessive water for five or six days, a trip to the veterinarian is in order. Make your appointment and tell the receptionist why you need an appointment right away.

The veterinarian will ask you the following questions:

- When did he last eat a normal meal?
- How long has he had diarrhea or been vomiting?
- Has he eaten anything in the last 24 hours?
- Could he have eaten a toy or a piece of clothing or anything else unusual?
- Is he drinking more water than usual?

The veterinarian will check him over, take his temperature and pulse, listen to his heart, feel his stomach for any lumps, look at his gums and teeth for color and check his eyes and ears. He will probably also draw blood to run tests.

At the end of the examination, the vet may send your dog home with you with some antibiotics, take some x-rays, or keep the dog overnight for observation. Follow your veterinarian's instructions and you will find that very often your dog will be back to normal in a day or

Be especially attentive to your Rottie's comfort on hot days. Bring along water and let him drink often, and be sure he has access to a shady spot.

CHAPTER 9

two. In the meantime, feed him light meals and keep him quiet, perhaps confined to his crate.

Parasites can be a problem, and there are certain ones of which you should be aware. Heartworm can be a deadly problem, and dogs in some parts of the country can be more prone to this than others. Heart-worms become very massive and wrap themselves around the dog's heart. If not treated, the dog will eventually die. In the spring, call your veterinarian and ask if your dog

Ticks are most prevalent in wooded areas. They pose danger to pets and humans alike, as they can transmit serious diseases like Lyme disease and Rocky Mountain spotted fever.

should have a heartworm test. If so, take him to the clinic and he will be given a test to make certain that he is clear of heartworm, and then he will be put on heartworm medication. This is important, particularly if you live in areas where mosquitoes are present.

Fleas are also a problem but particularly in the warmer parts of the country. You can purchase flea powder or a collar from the pet shop or ask your veterinarian what he suggests that you use. If you suspect fleas, lay your dog on his side, separate the coat to the skin and see if you see any skipping, jumping or skittering around of little bugs.

Ticks are more prevalent in areas where there are numerous trees. Ticks are small (to start) and dark, and they like to attach themselves to the warm parts of the ear, the leg pits, the face folds, etc. The longer they stay on the dog, the bigger they become, filling themselves with your pet's blood and becoming as big as a dime. Take your forceps and carefully pull the tick out to make sure you get the pincers. Promptly flush the

to raise a healthy dog. Always ask your vet what shots or medications your dog is getting and what they are for. Keep a notebook or dog diary and record all health information so you won't forget it. Believe me, you will forget.

Pups do need time to rest, but a lethargic puppy is an anomaly. If your pup lacks energy or seems uninterested in play, it's time for a visit to the vet to determine the problem.

tick down the toilet or light a match to it. Put alcohol on the wound and a dab of antibiotic salve.

Let common sense and a good veterinarian be your guides in coping with health problems. A well-informed dog owner is better prepared

Fortunately today's veterinary community is focused on preventative care and canine wellness as well as treating animals after they are sick. The American Holistic Veterinary Medical Association and other specialty groups now offer

CHAPTER 9

acupuncture, herbal remedies, homeopathy and other alternative therapies in addition to traditional disease treatment and prevention. Many pet owners today incorporate both philosophies in their dogs' health-care programs. You can learn more about these alternative natural-care disciplines through books or on the Internet, for talking to vets who have experience with holistic medicine.

Well-dog examinations are the foundation of preventative health care, and your Rottweiler should visit his veterinarian annually. Most importantly, an annual visit keeps your vet apprised of your pet's health progress, and the hands-on exam often turns up small or internal abnormalities you can't see or feel.

The Rottie's deep chest predisposes him to a potentially fatal condition called gastric torsion (or, more commonly, bloat). Bloat is directly related to feeding and exercise practices and is preventable through simple daily precautions. Ask your vet about how to protect your dog.

Your Rottweiler's health is in your hands between those annual visits to the veterinarian. Be ever-conscious of any changes in his appearance or behavior. Things to consider:

Has your Rottweiler gained a few too many pounds or suddenly lost weight? Are his teeth clean and white, or does he need some plaque attackers? Is he urinating more frequently, drinking more water than usual? Does he strain during a bowel movement? Are there any changes in his appetite? Does he appear short of breath, lethargic, overly tired? Have you noticed limping or signs of joint stiffness? These are all signs of serious health problems that you should discuss with your vet as soon as they appear. This is especially important for the senior dog, since even subtle changes can be a sign of something serious. The important thing is that you know your dog so you will be able to detect when he's not himself.

HOME CARE FOR YOUR ROTTIE

Overview

- Have a well-stocked doggie first-aid kit and be prepared in case of an emergency.
- Stay current with your dog's regular trips to the vet. Healthy adult dogs usually visit their vets for checkups annually.
- You are your dog's dentist in between checkups.
- Recognize signs of illness and visit the vet right away.
- Learn about parasites and how to control them.
- Your Rottweiler's health is in your hands. Be conscious of any changes in his behavior.

Feeding Your Rottweiler

Nutrition for your puppy is actually very easy. Dog-food companies hire many scientists and spend millions of dollars on research to determine what will be a healthy diet for your dog. Your breeder should have been feeding a premium puppy food and you should continue on with the same brand. As the dog matures you will change over to the adult formula of the same dog-food brand. Do not add vitamins or anything else unless your

Adults and puppies require different diets. Your breeder and vet can advise you about the proper age to make the switch, as well as changes in amounts and the frequency of meals as your Rottie reaches adulthood.

veterinarian suggests that you do so. Do not think that, by cooking up a special diet, you will turn out a product that is more nutritional than what the dog-food companies are providing.

Your young puppy will probably be fed three times a day and perhaps as many as four times a day. As he starts growing, you will cut his meals to two times a day, in the morning and in the evening. By the time he reaches eight months of age you will be changing over to the adult type of dog food. You can check your dog-food container for the amount, per pound of weight, that you should be feeding your dog. To the dry kibble, you will add water to moisten and possibly a tablespoon or so of a canned dog food for flavor. Avoid feeding "people food" treats, as some, like chocolate and onions, are toxic to dogs. A dog treat now and then will certainly be enjoyed. Keep a good covering of flesh over his ribs,

"Fill 'er up!" This hungry puppy looks ready for dinnertime.

A good after-dinner chew helps reduce plaque and contributes to overall dental health. Some toys are designed with bumps to massage the dog's gums and scrape his teeth as he chews.

but do not let your dog become a fat boy! However, the more active the dog, the more calories he will need. Always have fresh drinking water available. This may include a dish of water in the kitchen and another outside in the yard.

Bloat, in which a dog's stomach twists around and blocks anything from entering or exiting, can kill a dog in short order. The condition is related to feeding, eating and exercise habits and is most common in deep-chested breeds like the Rottweiler. Elevating the dog's bowls, restricting exercise in the hours before and after meals and never allowing him to gulp food or water are among the preventatives. Get the detailed list of precautions and symptoms from your veterinarian.

Your dog should always have a bowl of clean fresh water available. This is as important to his health as proper nutrition.

There are bowls made to attach to the dog's crate, although food and water in the crate is not a good idea before a pup is housebroken.

FEEDING YOUR ROTTWEILER

Overview

- Offering a top-quality dog food appropriate for your Rottie's stage of life is the most reliable and convenient way to provide complete nutrition for your dog.
- Discuss with your vet and/or breeder the amount to feed your Rottie, a feeding schedule and how to make changes as the dog matures.
- Bloat is a life-threatening condition that affects deep-chested dogs. It is related to eating and feeding habits and can be prevented.
- Your Rottweiler's health relies upon a proper diet.

Grooming Your Rottweiler

Introduce your pup to brushing with gentle strokes, using a soft bristle or wire pin brush.

Do understand before purchasing your dog that he will need some grooming and attention to his hygiene. However, a big plus with the Rottie is that there is a very minimal amount of grooming required, unlike with a Poodle or some other heavily coated breed.

A brush with soft to medium bristles is recommended to keep your dog's coat looking shiny and clean. Usually, a weekly brushing will do the trick, and a suitable brush can be purchased from your local pet-supply store. A mitt that fits over your hand, that is smooth on one side with soft wire pins on the other side, is excellent for the Rottweiler. When the undercoat drops, usually in the spring, you may need a comb or "rake" for removing the loose undercoat. A bath is certainly recommended when your dog is very dirty, but often a rubdown with a damp cloth will be ample for cleaning. Frequent bathing will deprive the dog's coat of important oils, drying the skin and coat. In general, baths are recommended twice a year, in the spring and the fall.

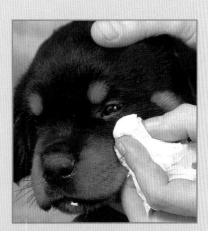

Tear stains and debris around the eyes can be wiped away gently with a damp soft cloth.

It is important to trim your dog's toenails and it is best to start this within a week of bringing your pup home. Purchase a quality toenail trimmer for pets. You may want to purchase a styptic stick in case you trim the nail too short and bleeding starts. Since Rottweilers have dark toenails, it is a bit more difficult to see

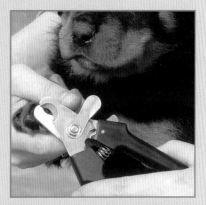

It is best to introduce your Rottie to nail clipping as a puppy, as you will have quite a difficult time trying to handle an adult Rottweiler who objects to his pedicures.

the blood vessel that runs inside the nail. You may nick the blood vessel until you are more familiar with trimming the nails. If you do not start trimming the nails at a young age so that your Rottie is used to this, you will have greater difficulty as the dog becomes larger, heavier and more difficult to hold.

If you give your dog treats of hard dog biscuits and bones to chew on, you will only have to have his teeth cleaned once a year at the

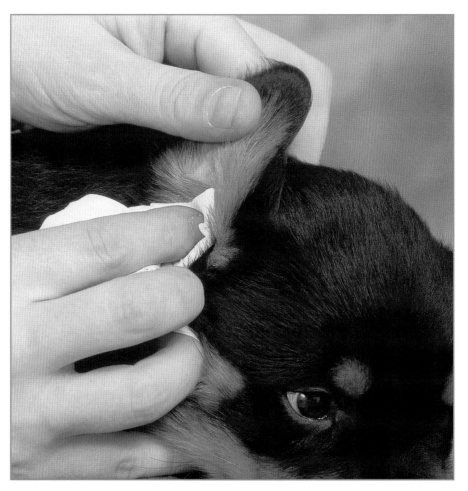

Inspect your pup's ears at each grooming session, checking for dirt, evidence of ear mites or any other signs of trouble. Clean the ears as needed using a soft cotton ball or wipe and an ear-cleansing solution.

vet's. During the other 364 days of the year, you will have to be your Rottweiler's dentist. Purchase a doggy toothbrush and toothpaste at your pet shop. Do not use human toothpaste, as it can harm the dog's teeth. Get your dog used to having his teeth brushed when he is still a puppy—wrestling a full-grown Rottweiler with a toothbrush in your hand will quickly become a Battle Royale that you will lose every time!

The Rottweiler, all in all, is a "wash and wear" dog. . .

easy to groom. Give him at least a weekly coat brushing, trim his toenails every month, clean his teeth weekly or so and wipe him down with a damp cloth when he looks like he needs it. Check his ears for mites and bad odors. Wipe them out with a damp cloth and a solution of hydrogen peroxide and white vinegar. Give him a bath only when it is necessary. You will now have a good-looking dog that you can be proud to be seen with!

GROOMING YOUR ROTTWEILER

Overview

- While the Rottweiler is an easy keeper as regards grooming, proper coat maintenance is a vital part of his overall health-care program and must be initiated when the pup is young.
- The Rottie owner must also tend to his dog's nails and ears.
- You will have to bathe your Rottweiler only occasionally, as too-frequent bathing is not good for the skin and coat.
- You will need only basic grooming equipment for your Rottie, such as a brush, an undercoat rake, nail clippers, stypic pencil, ear cleanser, cotton balls and doggie dental-care products.

Keeping Your Rottie Active

Many owners and their dogs are looking for challenging things to do, and there are many activities to keep you and your Rottie very busy, active and interested.

Rottweilers can excel in many activities because of their intelligence, their willingness to please, their tenacity and their athleticism. After puppy kindergarten, you may want to work toward a Canine Good Citizen® award. This is a program that, when successfully

Some Rotties used for herding are farm dogs and get to meet all kinds of interesting friends.

completed, shows that your dog will mind his manners at home, in public places and with other dogs. This class is available to dogs (pure-bred or otherwise) of any age and it's a fun, useful course for everyday life. There are ten steps, including: accepting a friendly stranger, sitting politely for petting, accepting light grooming and examination from a stranger, walking on a loose lead, coming when called, responding calmly to another dog, responding to distractions, down on command and remaining calm when the owner is out of sight for three minutes. Upon successful completion, your Rottie will receive an AKC Canine Good Citizen® certificate.

Conformation showing is perhaps the most popular type of canine competition among all breeds.

Once you've completed basic training, whether at home or in a class, you may like to progress to training for a sport. Obedience is an old sport at which the Rottweiler excels. Obedience trials are held either by themselves or in

The Rottweiler as a water retriever? You never know! Try out different activities to see what your versatile Rottie enjoys.

conjunction with an AKC dog show. There are many levels, starting with Novice, whereupon completion of three passing "legs," the dog will earn a Companion Dog (CD) title. The courses then continue in difficulty with Open at the second level. In the Open level, the dog includes off-lead work, silent hand signals, and picking the right dumbbells from a group of dumbbells. Not many dogs reach this level, and it is a major accomplishment for both owner and dog when a Utility degree is achieved.

Agility competition,

Up and over the A-frame, one of the obstacles in an agility trial.

earns a Companion Dog Excellent (CDX) upon completion of three successful legs. The next class is Utility (UD), which started in England, is a fairly new sport in America and can be easily found at dog shows. Look for the large, noisy ring filled with competitors and dogs running the course and excited spectators watching at ringside, joining in with cheers.

In agility training, dogs are taught to run an obstacle course that includes hurdles, ladders, jumps and a variety of other challenges. There are a number of degrees in agility, depending upon the obstacles that the dog is able to conquer. AKC defines agility as, "The enjoyment of bringing together communication, training, timing, accuracy and just plain fun in the ultimate game for you and your dog." Plus, it provides

The agile Rottweiler clears a bar jump with ease.

lots of exercise for both dog and owner.

The ultimate in degrees is the Versatile Companion Dog. This title recognizes those dogs and handlers who have been successful in multiple dog sports. In order to excel at any of the afore-mentioned activities, it is essential to belong to a dog club where there are equipment and facilities for practice. Find a good school in your area and attend a class as a spectator before enrolling. If you like the facility, the instructor and the type of instruction, sign your dog up for the next series of lessons. Classes are typically held two times a week.

Dog sports have become so popular with the public that there should be little difficulty in finding a training facility. You will find it a great experience, to work with your dog and meet new people with whom you will have a common interest. This will all take time and interest on your part, and a willing dog working on the other end of the leash.

Cart pulling goes back to the early days of the Rottweiler in Germany when he pulled the cart containing milk cans, meat or other supplies to the market. If ambitious, you can make a smart cart for your dog to pull youngsters around in. Be sure to have a proper harness for your dog when doing this activity. Again, your local Rottweiler club can tell you where to purchase this harness.

Schutzhund is another sport for which Rottweilers are well suited. Started in Germany, this is a sport that demands the best from your dog. These are not attack dogs, as some think, but dogs that are trained for courage, intelligence and sound temperament. When

Agility training can begin at around one year of age. Here a Rottie learns to balance over the dog walk.

taking up this sport with your dog, it is absolutely essential that you attend a reputable class with qualified trainers.

Of course, the easiest way to keep your dog active and fit is to take him for a walk every morning and

The Rottie returns, dumbbell in mouth, to hand off to the handler.

Obedience exercises include retrieving a dumbbell. The Rottweiler sits and waits for the throw.

evening, and this will also be good for you! Playing games with your dog will delight him. Chasing a ball or tugging on knotted socks is always great fun for a puppy or dog. Rottweilers have very strong jaws and

teeth, so you need the best of rubber toys to have them last more than one or two play sessions. Never give him a toy or ball that is small enough for him to swallow as, like a child, he will swallow it and an expensive trip to the veterinarian may follow.

Rotties are working dogs

and love to have work to do! At the American Rottweiler Club's national specialty, the following activities are offered for the breed, in addition to the conformation show: obedience trials, tracking tests, herding tests and trials, agility trials, variable surface tracks and carting competitions. Of all the national breed clubs, there are very few that offer this many activities, which shows how very versatile our Rottweiler is!

If you choose to engage your Rottweiler in Schutzhund training, you must have the proper equipment and the assistance of a professional trainer with experience in this discipline.

KEEPING YOUR ROTTIE ACTIVE

Overview

- The most basic activities for your Rottweiler are daily walks and free running time in a safely enclosed area. Daily walks reinforce that special bond between you and your Rottie.
- Consider enrolling in an obedience class to give your Rottweiler another fun outlet for his talents.
- Participating in dog shows, obedience trials and agility trials are excellent forums for dog and owner.
- The Rottweiler is eligible to participate in herding events, and he also is well suited to Schutzhund training and cart pulling.
- Rottie owners are fortunate to have a versatile breed, capable of a wide range of persuits.

ROTTWEILER

Your Rottie and His Vet

One of the most important things to do before bringing your puppy home is to find a good veterinarian. Your breeder, if from your area, should be able to recommend someone; otherwise, it will be your job to find a veterinarian that you like and trust.

Considerations for finding a veterinarian include finding someone, for convenience, who is within 10 miles of your home. Find a veterinarian that you like personally, and about whom you are confident

One of the first things you will do with your new puppy is bring him to the vet for an overall check-up and to set up a vaccination program.

regarding skills and ability with the Rottie. Visit the office to see that it looks and smells clean. It is your right to check on fees before setting up an appointment, and you will usually need an appointment. If you have a satisfactory visit, take the business card so that you have the clinic's number and the name of the veterinarian that you saw. Try to see the same vet at each visit, as he will personally know the history of your dog and your dog will be familiar with him.

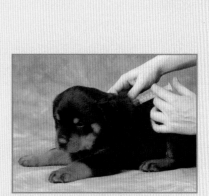

Bring health records from the breeder to show to your vet, as this will enable him to determine what shots the pup has already received and how he should continue.

Inquire whether the clinic takes emergency calls and, if they do not, as many no longer do, get the name, address and telephone number of the emergency veterinary service in your area and keep this with your veterinarian's phone number.

On your first visit, take along the documentation that your breeder gave you with a record of the shots that your puppy had so that the veteri-

You want to select a gentle vet who has experience with the Rottweiler and who makes your puppy feel at ease.

narian will know which series of shots your pup should be getting. You should also take in a fecal sample for a worm test.

VACCINES

The vaccines in booster shots can vary, and a single

essary and can negatively compromise a puppy's immature immune system.

The vaccines most commonly recommended by the America Veterinary Medical Association (AVMA) are those that protect against the diseases most

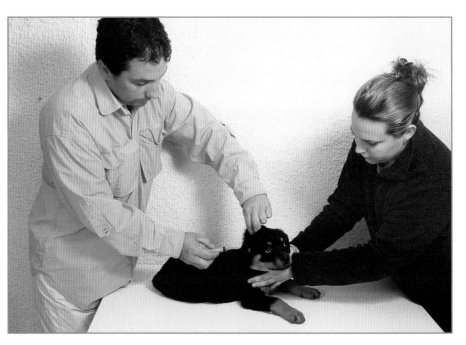

Be reassuring to your pup during his first trips to the vet. Treat rewards and praise will help him equate veterinary visits with good things.

injection may contain five, six, seven or even eight vaccines in one injection. Many breeders and veterinarians feel that some of those vaccines are unnec-

dangerous to your puppy and adult dog. These include distemper (canine distemper virus–CDV), fatal in puppies; canine parvovirus (CPV or parvo), highly contagious and also fatal in puppies and at-risk dogs; canine adenovirus (CAV2), highly contagious and high risk for pups under 16 weeks of age; canine hepatitis (CA1), highly contagious with pups at high risk; and rabies, which can be fatal.

Other vaccines no longer routinely recommended by the AVMA, except when the risk is present, are canine parainfluenza, leptospirosis, canine coronavirus, Bordetella (canine cough) and Lyme (borreliosis). These diseases are not considered fatal or high risk except in certain areas or circumstances. Your veterinarian can help you sort through the vaccine puzzle and also will alert you if there is an incidence of these diseases in your area so you can vaccinate accordingly.

The annual vaccination protocols that have been standard practice for

decades are currently under scrutiny. The AVMA has revised its vaccine guidelines and is now recommending vaccinating every three years instead of annually. Those guidelines are further supported by the American Animal Hospital Association, the American College of Veterinary Internal Medicine and other professional veterinary

The vet will examine the puppy's eyes to make sure they are clear and healthy. All puppies should come from parents that have been tested for and cleared of any genetic disorders of the eye.

associations. Mindful of the new guidelines, the revised AVMA brochure on vaccinations further suggests that veterinarians and owners consider a dog's individual immunization needs when planning his vaccination schedule. Many dog owners now do titer tests to check their dog's antibodies rather than automatically vaccinating for parvo or distemper.

The wisest and most prudent course is to administer only one shot in a single visit, rather than two or three (i.e., booster shot and rabies or other shot) at the same time. That means extra trips to your veterinarian with your puppy and adult dog, but your Rottie's healthy immune system is worth your time.

Rabies vaccination is mandatory in all 50 states. For many years the rabies vaccine has been available in a one-year and a three-year vaccine. Both offer the same protection, so why vaccinate every year? Check with your state statutes to find out if the three-year vaccine is legal in your state.

Once a serious concern for Rottweilers, parvovirus is recognized by fever, vomiting and diarrhea. This is a deadly disease for pups and can spread very easily through their feces. The vaccine is highly effective in prevention. Distemper, at one time, was the scourge of dog breeding, but with the proper immunization and a clean puppy-rearing area, this no longer presents a problem to the reputable breeder. Canine hepatitis, very rare in the United States, is a severe liver infection caused by a virus. Leptospirosis is an uncommon disease that affects the kidneys; it is rare in young puppies, occurring primarily in adult dogs.

What is lurking in the grass that may find itself a home in your Rottie's coat? Inspect your dog's coat after time spent outdoors, and use your grooming sessions to check all the way down to the skin for lumps, bumps, parasites or other problems.

CHAPTER 3

HEALTH CONCERNS

The Rottweiler is a relatively healthy dog, but there are some problems within the breed of which you should be aware. Hip dysplasia is a major concern, as it is in other large breeds. Hip dysplasia is an inherited disease in which the head of the femur (thigh bone) fails to fit into the socket in the hip bone and there is not enough muscle mass to hold the joint together. This can often be a very painful problem for the dog, causing him to limp or to move about with great difficulty. Treatment methods range from therapeutic to surgical, depending on severity.

All Rottweilers that are bred should have normal hips as determined by an x-ray and approved by the Orthopedic Foundation for Animals (OFA). Rotweilers also can have an incidence of elbow dysplasia, which is also a hereditary disease. Again, x-rays should be taken of the animals that are to be bred and, if normal, these results will also be registered by the OFA.

Osteochondrosis dissecans (OCD) is a problem for young and fast-growing dogs in the larger breeds. Degeneration can occur, particularly in the forelegs of large dogs. The most commonly affected areas are the shoulders, elbows, hocks and knees.

Rottweilers can have a heart problem called sub-aortic stenosis, which can be either a very mild or severe disorder. This congenital disorder causes the aorta to narrow, due to scar tissue, restricting the flow of blood and hardening the heart. Severely affected dogs may show no symptoms and then die suddenly. It is thought to be hereditary; thus affected dogs or those determined to be carriers of the gene should not be bred.

Eye diseases include the eyelids' moving inward (entropion) or rolling for problems. If found clear of these diseases, the dogs will be registered with the Canine Eye Registration Foundation (CERF). CERF keeps a comprehensive database of all Rottweilers

Be sure to see clearances that prove the parents' orthopedic health before purchasing a pup. Also follow the breeder's and vet's recommendations for safe exercise, as a large-breed puppy needs special care while developing.

outward (ectropion). Both conditions are inherited and will require surgical correction. The Rottweiler can also have several other inherited eye diseases that can impair sight. As with the hips and elbows, the eyes of dogs to be used for breeding should be tested that have been tested for the various eye diseases. This is a vital resource for breeders and pet buyers alike.

Other problems include cancer, which can be found in any breed, hypothyroidism, epilepsy and skin problems. You should be aware of these problems within the breed and ask the breeder if he has had his dogs tested. If he has, ask to see certificates of clearance with the appropriate registries. Do not just accept the breeder's word that the sire and dam of the litter have been tested for these various problems. This list may seem daunting, but responsible breeders will have had their stock tested and will be doing their best to eliminate these problems in the breed.

Health guarantees are important, and a responsible breeder will give you a contract that will guarantee your pup against certain congenital defects. This guarantee will be limited in time to six months or one year. If there is a problem, he will possibly replace the

You love your Rottweiler and want to share as many years as possible together. Show him how much he means to you by always paying careful attention to his health and getting him proper and regular veterinary care.

pup or offer some refund in his price.

A last note: you may or may not want to consider neutering your Rottweiler, or the breeder may *require* neutering. A neutered male will be less aggressive, less likely to lift his leg in the house and have less of a tendency to mount other dogs (or your leg). A neutered female will not come into season every six months, which is not only very hard on your house but will attract neighboring dogs.

Despite the potential problems in the breed, overall the Rottie is a hardy breed of dog.

YOUR ROTTIE AND HIS VET

Overview

- Before you pick up your puppy, select a qualified vet. Upon bringing your Rottie home, take him to the vet for an exam.
- At the first visit, your vet will confirm your pup's good health and set up his vaccination schedule.
- Discuss with your vet the best and safest vaccination program.
- Discuss with your breedfer all breed-specific problems and see proof that your puppy's parents are free of those conditions.
- All aspects of spaying/neutering and how to protect your Rottie from bloat are health issues to research and talk about with your vet.

CHAPTER 14

Your Aging Rottweiler

Many Rottweilers stay active and alert well into their senior years.

As your dog ages, he will start to slow down. He will not play as hard or as long as he used to and he will sleep more. He will find the sunbeam in the morning hours and take long naps. At this time, you will probably put him on a senior-formula dog food. Continue to watch his weight, as it is more important than ever not to let your Rottweiler become obese in his senior years. You will notice that his muzzle will become gray and you may see opacites in his eyes, signs of cataracts. And as he becomes older, he may become arthritic.

Continue your walks, making them shorter, and give him a baby aspirin when he appears to be stiff. Keep up with your grooming, as both of you will like to have him looking and smelling clean. Watch for lumps and bumps and take him to the veterinarian if you are concerned. Incontinence can also become a problem with the older dog. This is frustrating for you and hard on the house, but he hasn't become "unhousebroken"; rather, his excretory muscle control is fading.

Veterinary care has changed much over the last decade or two, as has medical care for humans. Your veterinarian can now do much to extend your dog's life if you want to spend the money. While this will extend his life, it will not bring back your Rottie's youth. Your primary

Your older Rottie may have trouble doing certain things that never posed a problem, like getting himself into the car, and may need your help.

He may slow down in his activities, but the older Rottie benefits from less vigorous exercise and will enjoy the time spent with his favorite person.

concern should be to help your pet live out his life comfortably, and there are medications that can be helpful for this goal. Whatever you decide, try to put your dog's well-being and comfort ahead of your emotions and do what will be best for your pet. Keep things as consistent as possible, and realize that his senses are not as keen as they used to be. Make allowances and adjustments for your senior citizen, and help make his life as easy as you can. Most of all, be patient with your Rottweiler and the changes that occur with age.

When the end inevitably comes, always remember the many wonderful years that your pet gave to you and your family. With that thought, it may not be long before you are looking for a new puppy for the household. And there you are, back at the beginning, with a cute bundle of joy, ready for another ten years or more of happiness!

YOUR AGING ROTTWEILER

Overview

- Your older dog's activity level will decrease as he ages.
- Keep an eye on your senior dog's diet and weight, as obesity is especially harmful to older dogs.
- Graying, eye problems and arthritis are common in senior dogs.
- Keep up with your Rottweiler's regular routines, compensating for the changes that accompany aging.
- Give your senior Rottweiler the best veterinary care that you can, as well as the good care and affection that you've shown him all his life.